# Great
# BRIDGE
## Designs

BY SOPHIE WASHBURNE

Cavendish
Square

NEW YORK

Published in 2023 by Cavendish Square Publishing, LLC
29 East 21st Street, New York, NY 10010

Website: cavendishsq.com

Disclaimer: Portions of this work were originally authored by Kathy Furgang and published as
*21st-Century Bridges*. All new material this edition authored by Sophie Washburne.

Cataloging-in-Publication Data
Names: Washburne, Sophie.
Title: Great bridge designs / Sophie Washburne.
Description:  New York : Cavendish Square, 2023. | Series: Engineering
wonders of the 21st century | Includes glossary and index.
Identifiers: ISBN 9781502665249 (pbk.) | ISBN 9781502665256 (library bound) | ISBN 9781502665263 (ebook)
Subjects: LCSH: Bridges--Design and construction--Juvenile literature.
Classification: LCC TG300.W37 2023 | DDC 624.2--dc23

Editor: Jennifer Lombardo
Copyeditor: Michelle Denton
Designer: Rachel Rising

The photographs in this book are used by permission and through the courtesy of: Cover Aerial-motion/Shutterstock.
com; cover, pp. 1–48 (gears) Artistdesign29/Shutterstock.com; cover, pp. 1–48 (grid) Cesar Termulo Jr/Shutterstock.
com; cover, pp. 1–48 (boxes) Olessia_Art/Shutterstock.com; p. 4 HilaryJane17/Shutterstock.com; p. 6 Reuben Teo/
Shutterstock.com; p. 7 Rabbitmindphoto/Shutterstock.com; p. 8 Vladimir Krupenkin/Shutterstock.com; p. 10
Nasky/Shutterstock.com; p. 12 Amphi/Shutterstock.com; p. 14 VRP Photography/Shutterstock.com; p. 17 S.Borisov/
Shutterstock.com; p. 20 u3d/Shutterstock.com; p. 22 World History Archive/Alamy Stock Photo; p. 23 Mohammad Fahmi
Abu Bakar/Shutterstock.com; p. 25 Jaromir Chalabala/Shutterstock.com; p. 26 https://commons.wikimedia.org/wiki/
File:Broughton-suspension-bridge.jpg; p. 28 imagoDens/Shutterstock.com; p. 31 solkafa/Alamy Stock Photo; p. 32 Andriy
Solovyov/Shutterstock.com; p. 35 framedbythomas/Shutterstock.com; p. 36 Orange Deer studio/Shutterstock.com; p. 38
Frolova_Elena/Shutterstock.com; p. 41 Situ Gupta/Shutterstock.com;
p. 43 muratart/Shutterstock.com.

Some of the images in this book illustrate individuals who are models. The
depictions do not imply actual situations or events.

CPSIA compliance information: Batch #CSCSQ23: For further information contact
Cavendish Square Publishing LLC, New York, New York, at 1-877-980-4450.

Printed in the United States of America

Find us on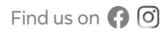

# CONTENTS

Some bridges have lasted for hundreds of years.

# Introduction

Bridges play an important role in transportation history. Without them, many places would be difficult or impossible to get to. People have been building bridges for thousands of years. The earliest bridges were often very short and simple—a way to easily get across a gap. Many of these bridges have fallen down over the years because people stopped maintaining them. For example, remains of bridges from the Mycenaean period have been found in Greece. These date back to about 1600 BCE. Other ancient bridges have stood the test of time. The oldest known bridge in the world that is still in use today crosses the Meles river in Turkey. It was built in 850 BCE.

As time passed and technology improved, people learned more about how to make bridges that would last for a long time. For example, the ancient Romans discovered that ground-up volcanic rock made a better material for binding rocks together than dirt, which could be washed away in heavy rain. The Romans were also famous for building aqueducts. An aqueduct is a bridge across a valley or other large gap of land. One end

Moon bridges such as this one are common in China. They are highly arched so their reflection will look like the full moon.

of the bridge is higher than the other, making it slanted. A channel is made in the bridge so water can flow from the top of the aqueduct to the bottom. This delivers water from a higher location to a lower location. Aqueducts were very helpful in the large Roman Empire. For example, crops could be grown farther away from water sources because the aqueduct delivered the water to them. Today, there are Roman-built aqueducts all over Europe because of how far Roman control extended.

Early bridges were mostly made out of stone or wood. Later, engineers found that other materials, such as concrete and steel, were better. Concrete is made by mixing cement with water and **aggregates** such as sand or crushed stone. These extra ingredients make it very strong and durable, so a concrete bridge can last for years. Steel is made by mixing iron and carbon. It is lightweight, but also very strong. Concrete and steel are the main building materials for almost every bridge built today. Other advancements in technology have helped people build bridges that are incredibly long or that move out of the way of large boats. Some bridges are built to be beautiful as well as useful. Amazing improvements may be made in the future that change the way bridges are built, but one thing is certain: Bridges will never go out of style.

This ancient aqueduct was built by the Romans in what is now the country of Spain.

The length of the gap a bridge needs to cross is an important part of deciding which style of bridge should be used.

# CHAPTER ONE

# Types of Bridges

The people who design the things we use in everyday society—including roads, tunnels, buildings, airports, dams, and bridges—are called civil engineers. The word "civil" here refers to things **civilians** use, rather than the military. There are several different kinds of bridges, and civil engineers need to think about a lot of things when deciding what kind of bridge to build somewhere: How often will it be used? How heavy will the things that cross it be? What kind of ground will it be built on? Will it cross water or a mountain valley? All of these questions and more must be answered before a civil engineer can decide which type of bridge is the best one for a particular project.

All bridges need to balance the forces of compression and tension. Compression is a squeezing force, while tension is a pulling force. When a load presses down on a bridge, the top of the bridge pushes toward the center (compression), while

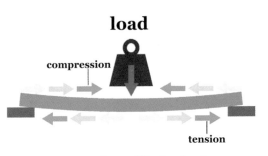

A concrete beam will begin to bend when heavily loaded.

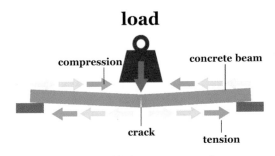

The base of the beam starts to crack where the concrete is pulled apart.

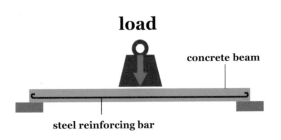

Placing a steel rod inside the beam holds the concrete together and stops the beam from cracking.

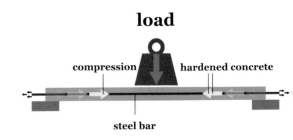

Stretching the rod and then releasing it to squeeze the concrete makes the beam very strong.

This diagram illustrates one way engineers can strengthen a concrete bridge.

the bottom of the bridge pulls away from the center (tension). If there is too much of either force, the bridge will break. Supports underneath or on top of a bridge can help balance these two forces.

# USING BEAMS FOR SUPPORT

A beam bridge is the simplest type of bridge. It is simply a roadway sitting on top of supports. A short beam bridge may

# A Team Effort

There are many people who work on different stages of bridge building. The first people involved survey the land. Their job is to do tests and make measurements to find out what the soil is made of, how deep and strong it is, and other information. This information helps engineers figure out things such as what materials to use and what kind of bridge should be built. They use computer-aided design (CAD) programs to make a model of the bridge. This helps them identify and fix problems before the bridge is built. They can use the CAD software to simulate different situations, such as extreme weather or weight, and see how the bridge will stand up to them.

After the bridge is designed, crews clear the land and make it ready for building. Construction crews may work nonstop for years to make a structure as large as a bridge. They work under the guidance of engineers and construction foremen or forewomen who check their work. The work does not stop after the bridge is open to the public. Bridges need to be constantly inspected to make sure they are safe. Repair crews may work on repairs while the bridge is open to the public.

need supports only on the ends of the bridge. Longer bridges may have supports at set distances. These supports hold the weight of the traffic across the bridge. The weight that is added to the beam of the bridge—whether it is cars, **pedestrians**, or animals—is called the load. The more supports a beam bridge has underneath, the greater the load the bridge can hold.

Sometimes a simple beam bridge, such as this one in Switzerland, can get the job done.

For a simple path across a roadway or narrow waterway, a beam bridge can provide all the support needed. Many beam bridges have weight limits so the load is not more than the bridge roadway and supports can handle. To support heavier loads, other bridge types are needed.

## A STRONG SHAPE

Builders have been constructing arch bridges for thousands of years. An arch bridge has a roadway that is supported by an arch underneath it. The semicircular shape underneath the bridge helps distribute the load to the two supports, called abutments, on either end. This allows the structure to spread the force of the load to the ends. When a force is applied to the top of the roadway as traffic passes over, the weight of that load is transferred to the stronger ends.

The greater the length of the bridge, the more arches are needed to spread out the load. The materials used are important too. For example, a stone arch bridge cannot support as much weight as a **reinforced** steel arch bridge. Some modern steel arch bridges can be more than 1,000 feet (305 meters) long with the support of only a single arch. This is because the weight of the building material adds to the load, and steel is much lighter than stone. As builders plan and design bridges, they must be able to predict the loads that will pass over the bridge. This helps them choose the right materials and designs for the length the bridge will be.

# GIVING EXTRA SUPPORT

A truss is a framework of connecting elements that gives extra support to a structure. Trusses are often made from a network of triangles. These give extra points of support to a square or rectangular structure. For example, if you make a cube out of popsicle sticks and place a large weight on top of it, the

The triangle shape of a truss adds to its strength.

cube may break. However, if you add extra popsicle sticks to connect the corners of the cube with ones diagonal from it, the structure becomes stronger. This extra support is called a truss. A structure with more trusses will be stronger. In a similar way, adding trusses to connect a bridge's supports makes the bridge stronger. When engineers need to reinforce an existing bridge, one option is to add trusses to spread out the load between the support points.

## SUSPENDED BETWEEN TOWERS

Another type of bridge is a suspension bridge. With this type, the bridge's roadway is supported by a series of cables suspended between tall towers. The towers anchor the bridge and provide many points of support. As a load pushes down on the bridge's roadway, the cables transfer the weight to the towers. The towers provide grounding, which means the force of the load is transferred into the ground to support the bridge.

There are many benefits to building suspension bridges. Getting support from cables means that fewer materials are needed for this type of bridge than other types, which makes them less expensive to build. The suspended cables also provide some flexibility for the roadway, making them less likely to break or snap during a light earthquake. However, the flexibility can also be a disadvantage because too much shaking, such as when there are high winds, can make the roadway bend or break. This is why engineers must think about the kind of weather a location gets when they are deciding what kind of bridge to build. A suspension bridge may be a good idea in a place that gets a lot of earthquakes but a bad idea in a place that gets a lot of hurricanes.

# KEPT IN PLACE WITH CABLES

Long cables that attach from a tower to the roadway secure cable-stayed bridges. A cable-stayed bridge may look somewhat like a suspension bridge, but the connections and supports are different. The cables connect directly from the tower to the roadway, and only one tower is needed to connect the cables. The cables are rigid and extend out in a pattern from the tower to the roadway. There are several different patterns engineers can choose from, including harp, fan, and star.

Cable-stayed bridges are a popular design among today's bridge engineers. The cables provide strong support and allow for interesting designs. For a very long bridge, multiple towers can be used along the roadway.

## UNDER THE BRIDGE

A cantilever bridge is one that uses horizontal structures that are supported on only one end. This type of bridge is useful for expanding the span between towers. This is especially useful for bridges that must have traffic run underneath them because there is more room for traffic underneath the bridge.

In some places, bridges have been built over waterways where boats frequently travel. Over the years, bigger boats have become common. To make sure boats can pass without getting stuck or breaking the bridge, some bridges have been built to move out of the way of the boats. This type of bridge is called a drawbridge. There are several different kinds, depending on the way they move. Swing bridges, as the name suggests, swing out of the way of boats. Bascule bridges have a lever system that raises one end of the bridge while lowering the other, the way a balance scale tips when weight is applied to it. In fact, the word "bascule" comes from the French word for a balance scale. Many bascule bridges have two of these lever systems— one for each half of the bridge. This makes the bridge look as if it is splitting in half.

Tower Bridge (*shown here*) in London, England, is one of the world's most famous drawbridges.

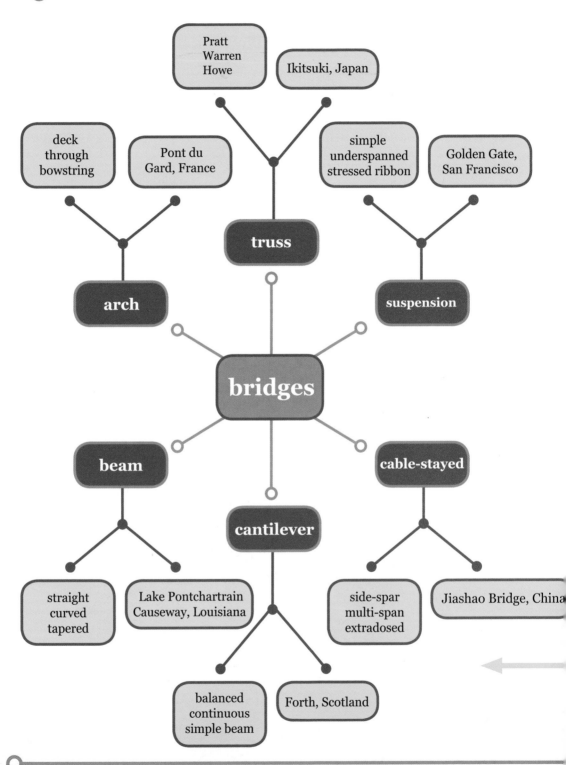

Pratt
Warren
Howe

Ikitsuki, Japan

deck
through
bowstring

Pont du
Gard, France

simple
underspanned
stressed ribbon

Golden Gate,
San Francisco

**truss**

**arch**

**suspension**

**bridges**

**beam**

**cable-stayed**

**cantilever**

straight
curved
tapered

Lake Pontchartrain
Causeway, Louisiana

side-spar
multi-span
extradosed

Jiashao Bridge, China

balanced
continuous
simple beam

Forth, Scotland

Cantilever bridges are often built either with steel trusses or concrete box **girders** to give them extra strength. Bridges frequently combine multiple building methods, making it harder to identify them as one specific type of bridge. Additionally, bridges can be grouped together in many different ways. Instead of building method, they could be organized by the type of load they are built for, the type of material they are made of, the way they look, and more. There are also multiple different ways to group each kind of bridge. For example, beam bridges alone can be grouped by their geometry, the shape of the supports, or where the supports are placed.

# THINK IT THROUGH

1. What kinds of classes do you think civil engineers need to take in school?
2. How does spreading out the load make a bridge stronger?
3. Why is a triangle a stronger shape than a square?

Within each category of bridge, there are smaller categories, or subcategories. This diagram shows three subcategories of each type of bridge as well as a famous example of each main type.

Engineers can use computers to make 3-D models such as this to test bridges before they are built.

# CHAPTER TWO

# Learning from Failure

Designing a bridge takes a lot of planning. Engineers need to think about the materials that would be best for the project and the exact measurements needed for the height and width of the bridge. They need to know the total weight of the maximum load that could pass over the bridge at one time. Instead of building the full bridge in the hope that their plan works, they build **prototypes** to test their plan. If the plan does not work, they can rework different parts to find a solution. Testing and redesigning new ideas is one of the most important parts of the process.

Even with all this testing, sometimes people find out after building a bridge that a certain material behaved in an unexpected way, or that they were mistaken about how much traffic would cross the bridge at one time. Engineers learn from their failures to make the next bridge even better.

# TRAGEDY IN WASHINGTON STATE

One of the most infamous bridge failures happened in Washington State in 1940, just a few months after the bridge opened to the public. The Tacoma Narrows Bridge was the third-longest bridge in the world when it opened to public traffic on July 1, 1940. The suspension bridge crossed over Puget Sound, cutting the drive from Tacoma, Washington, to the Kitsap Peninsula from 2.5 hours to just 11 minutes. The suspension bridge was designed to sway a little in high winds. This reduced

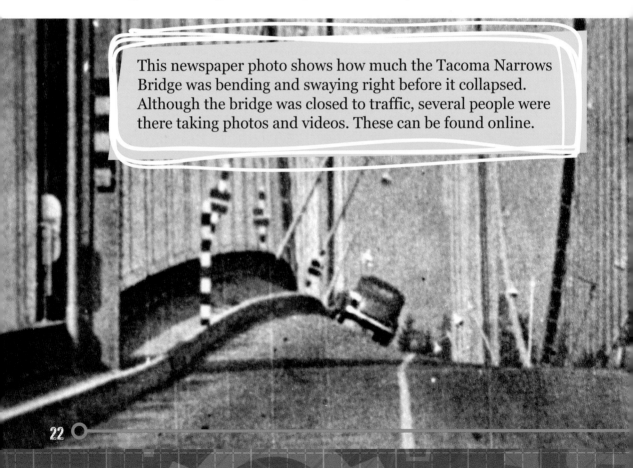

This newspaper photo shows how much the Tacoma Narrows Bridge was bending and swaying right before it collapsed. Although the bridge was closed to traffic, several people were there taking photos and videos. These can be found online.

# Building Over Water

Many bridges are designed and built to span large bodies of water. It is important for the towers or abutments of a bridge to be sunk deep into the ground below a river. There are several different ways a construction crew can do this. One is by using large airtight chambers called caissons. Some caissons can be put in place and immediately filled with concrete. For deeper water or more complicated construction work, workers may be lowered to the bottom of the caisson. Caissons are permanent structures; they end up becoming part of the bridge.

Another option is a cofferdam. Cofferdams serve the same function as caissons, but they are temporary and are removed when construction is done. Some cofferdams are simple—for example, a large piece of watertight fabric filled with water. Others require almost as much engineering work as the bridge itself. These involve placing **piles** at specific lengths in the floor of the body of water, then pumping the water out to leave an air-filled chamber in the middle of the water. Cofferdam construction crews must make sure the walls will not leak or collapse—or the workers inside may drown.

Shown here are workers making repairs at the bottom of a cofferdam.

strain that could cause the roadway to crack. However, the bridge moved much more than intended. People noticed this, but no one thought it was much of a problem.

On November 7, 1940, high winds began in the early morning. This caused the deck of the bridge to bounce and sway more than it ever had before. The steel and concrete waved, bounced, and eventually began to twist as the winds increased. The roadway was quickly closed to traffic as the problem became worse. Finally, at about 10:30 a.m., a section of the bridge's roadway dropped into the water. Soon, the entire bridge collapsed and fell into Puget Sound. Because traffic had been cleared, no one was injured in the incident. This accident taught engineers the importance of fixing problems as soon as they are noticed.

## ACCOUNTING FOR VIBRATIONS

Another important lesson in bridge building is learning the effects that different forces have on bridges. In 1831, soldiers marched across a bridge in England called the Broughton Suspension Bridge. Normally, when a group of people walk together, their feet hit the ground a few seconds before or after each other. However, the soldiers marched in step, meaning they all put their feet down at the same time. This created vibrations at the same **frequency** as the bridge's natural vibrations. This amplified the vibrations to a strength the bridge could not handle. As a result, the bridge quickly weakened and broke apart.

Although the lesson about amplified vibrations was important, it may not have been the whole story. The television show *MythBusters* set out to see if it could recreate the collapse of a bridge due to repeated vibrations. After failing to break apart their model bridge, the show's hosts concluded that the

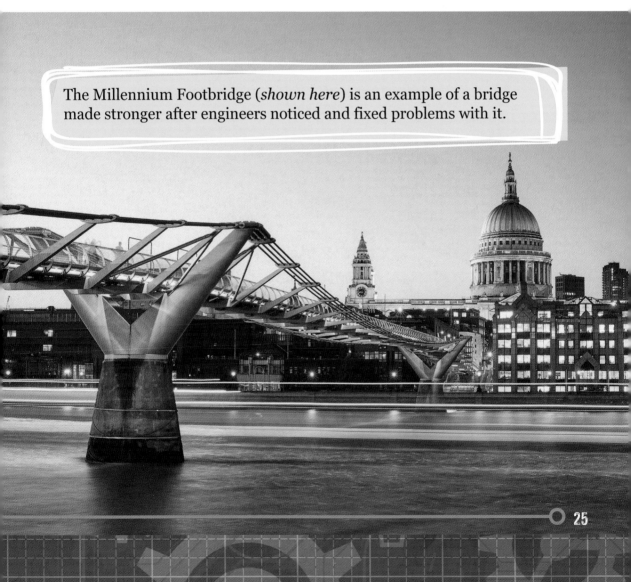

The Millennium Footbridge (*shown here*) is an example of a bridge made stronger after engineers noticed and fixed problems with it.

Broughton Suspension Bridge might have been in poor condition before the soldiers crossed it. They suspected that the extra force on the bridge weakened it further and made it collapse. This is why bridges need continued maintenance after they are built.

When the Millennium Footbridge opened in London, England, in 2000, a big celebration was planned. Crowds gathered for the opening of this new steel suspension bridge that crossed

The Broughton Suspension Bridge (*shown here*) taught engineers an important lesson.

the city's River Thames. However, the weight of the crowds made the bridge vibrate and sway from side to side slightly. Researchers later found that when a bridge sways sideways, people will unconsciously match their steps to the sway to keep their balance. This amplified the Millennium Footbridge's natural vibrations, similar to the problem that occurred when soldiers crossed the Broughton Suspension Bridge in 1831. The Millennium Bridge did not fall, but engineers had learned from the Tacoma Narrows Bridge not to ignore problems. They closed the bridge for nearly two years to reinforce it. Although the design of the bridge itself was not a problem, the Millennium Footbridge reminded engineers of how important it is to make adjustments based on the type of traffic a bridge will get.

# THINK IT THROUGH

1. Why does swaying a little bit help stop a bridge from cracking or breaking?
2. When would a cofferdam be a better choice than a caisson?
3. What kind of things do you think engineers need to think about when designing a bridge that cars drive over?

Shown here is the historic Kinzua railroad bridge in Pennsylvania after it was destroyed by a tornado. Experts later concluded that some of the bolts were so rusty they could not hold up against the wind. As extreme weather events increase due to climate change, keeping bridges in good working order will become even more important.

# CHAPTER THREE

# Planning Ahead

Civil engineers need to study a lot of different areas of science and math to build effective bridges. For example, **thermodynamics** is important because the climate of the places where bridges are built will influence the materials engineers choose for their projects. The types of steel, the connections between joints, and the length of time that materials last are also all important factors in planning for a strong bridge that will last well into the future.

Additionally, knowing about the climate change crisis has changed some things about the way new bridges are being built. For instance, extreme weather is happening more frequently all over the planet, so bridges must be built to stand up to more of these weather events. Engineers also need to think about climate-friendly ways to build bridges so they do not add to the problem.

# STANDING UP TO EARTHQUAKES

Earthquakes occur most often in areas where the plates of Earth's crust meet. These places must have the strongest bridges and structures. If a bridge is destroyed during an earthquake, the areas of land it connected may no longer be accessible. In some cases, there are longer routes people can take, but in others—for example, if the bridge was the only way on or off an island—people can be dangerously isolated.

The best thing engineers can do in areas where earthquakes are common is plan ahead. They use reinforced materials that can withstand strong shaking. This cuts down on repairs they might need to do after an earthquake. It could even save the entire structure from falling.

In 1989, an earthquake in San Francisco, California, damaged the eastern span of the San Francisco-Oakland Bay Bridge. After studying it, engineers decided it was best to replace that whole span of the bridge. The new bridge section would be expensive, but leaving it as it was would put lives in danger. Based on earthquake prediction data, scientists and engineers assumed the bridge would likely be hit with more earthquakes, so they had to make sure the bridge would be able to withstand them.

The suspension cables on the new span are reinforced by bundling hundreds of wire cables together to make a larger cable. Several of those bundled cables are also bunched together into one strong steel cable that can withstand great amounts of movement during an earthquake.

The base of the bridge is strong concrete and steel, with piles that extend almost 200 feet (61 m) into the bedrock under the bay. This gives extra support to the sections of bridge attached above it. In the event of a sudden or violent movement of the ground, the reinforced base of the bridge can help protect the entire structure.

# THINKING ABOUT THE ENVIRONMENT

The climate change crisis has affected the way engineers think about bridge building. An increase in hurricane or tornado

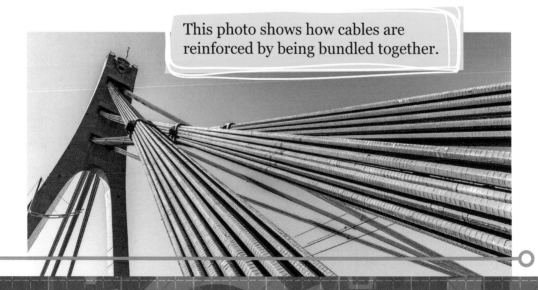

This photo shows how cables are reinforced by being bundled together.

activity, for example, requires that engineers build bridges that are stronger than ever. Flooding is also an important issue. Many bridges are built to be high enough for ships to travel underneath them. A permanent change in water levels due to rising temperatures would change the height that a bridge should be to allow ship traffic underneath. Engineers rely on precise calculations so the structure they are building fits within the environment. If the environment changes, engineers must be ready to problem-solve to make public structures safe.

Engineers also need to think about their own impact on the environment. For example, steel is a man-made product, but it comes from iron, which is a natural resource that has to be mined from the earth. Mining iron ore can be bad for the environment. It uses a lot of energy, and that energy generally comes from burning fossil fuels. When fossil fuels are burned,

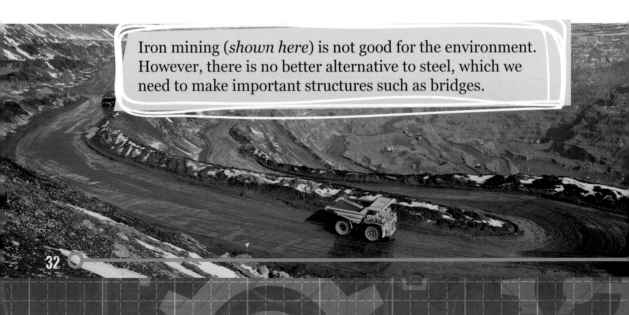

Iron mining (*shown here*) is not good for the environment. However, there is no better alternative to steel, which we need to make important structures such as bridges.

they produce **emissions** that pollute the air. Waste from iron ore mining can also pollute water sources.

Making the steel from the iron is also a process that can pollute the environment. Any factory process can create pollution over time, especially if factory owners resist changes that could make their factories more eco-friendly, or good for the environment, but also more expensive to run.

However, steel is still the most **sustainable** material to use for bridges. Unlike objects such as cars that will wear down and need to be recycled or thrown away within about 15 years, bridges are built to last for hundreds of years. Steel is durable and strong, but it is also lightweight. Lightweight materials are less damaging to the environment because less energy is used to create the materials. Furthermore, less of it needs to be used in construction than other materials, and what is used does not need to be replaced as often.

# EXPENSIVE BUT NECESSARY

Cost is a major factor for engineers because projects always have a budget they need to follow. They must consider the cost of everything: the land preparation, the materials used, the delivery of the materials, the construction, and more. Just fixing damage to bridges can cost more than $1 million. Making bridges from

# Planning for Road Traffic

When cars first appeared on roads, there was not as much worry about the weight of the traffic going over bridges. Fewer people had cars at that time, so there were no traffic jams, and there was rarely more than one car at a time crossing a bridge. As cars became more common, engineers had to build bridges to hold much more weight. If 50 cars cross a bridge roadway in half an hour, the bridge does not face the total load of those 50 cars all at once. However, if the 50 cars are stuck on the roadway in a traffic jam, the bridge must be strong enough to bear their total weight all at once.

The increase in the number of cars also makes it difficult to replace old bridges without causing major traffic problems. This is why engineers often work on building a new bridge right beside the old bridge. Cars continue to cross the old bridge until the new bridge is finished and opened to the public. When cars start driving on the new bridge, the old bridge is torn down. This is especially important in places where a bridge is the only way to get to or from an area.

the first designs through the opening of the structure can easily pass $1 billion.

Bridges are generally paid for by the government using taxes, and some people do not like the idea of spending so much on one thing. However, the building cost is not the whole story. The fewer repairs a bridge will need over time, the less it will cost on average. This is why engineers try to use the best materials available, even if it makes the bridge cost more to build. Additionally, bridges help make money, so that profit is balanced out against the cost. One way a bridge could be profitable is by helping truck drivers move goods from place to place more quickly; saving time would make the cost of those goods lower. Another is by connecting two places that have goods and services to exchange with each other. If the cost of building a bridge is $1 million, but it is unlikely to need many repairs over time and it will help an area make $2 million, it is considered a good investment.

# THINK IT THROUGH

1. What are some ways engineers could make bridges stand up to extreme weather such as hurricanes or tornadoes?

2. What are some ways to make steel production more eco-friendly?

3. Can you think of another way bridges could be worth the building cost?

With a price tag of $4.4 billion, the Great Belt Fixed Link (*shown here*) in Denmark is the most expensive bridge ever built. However, the Oakland Bay Bridge cost $1.3 billion to build in 1936 and $6.4 billion to repair after the 1989 earthquake, making it the bridge that has cost the most overall.

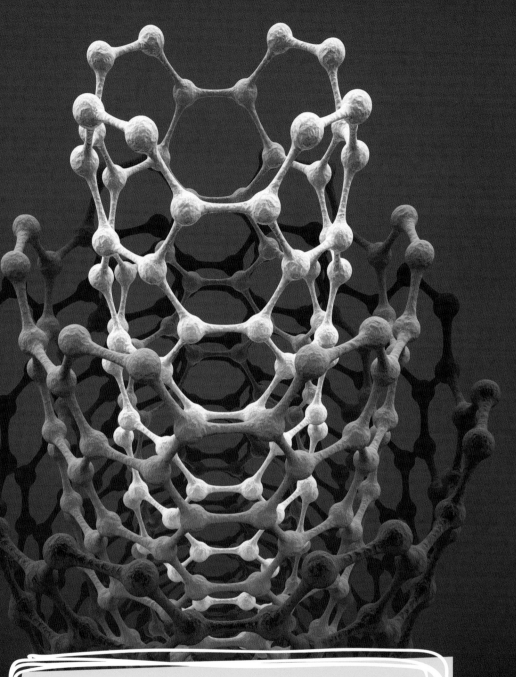

Carbon nanotubes are so small, the individual pieces can only be seen under a microscope. This picture shows what their structure looks like. Part of the reason they are so strong is because of the bonds between the molecules.

# CHAPTER FOUR

# Imagining the Future

New materials and technology are being invented all the time, and engineers have found ways to use some of them to make bridges even better. Strong materials, such as carbon **nanotubes**, will allow people to build bridges that are longer and higher than ever. Adding computer technology to bridges will help keep them in good repair, making them safer to use even after many years.

Some bridges are not only functional, but they are also works of art. Making bridges beautiful to look at can present an extra challenge for designers because whatever decorative features are added to the bridge must be just as strong and safe as the rest of the structure. However, getting it right can help a bridge add to the landscape where it is built instead of taking away from it.

# A BRIDGE FOR BOATS

In 2003, Germany opened the world's longest aqueduct for water traffic. It is called the Magdeburg Water Bridge, and it allows ships to cross above the Elbe River. Before the bridge was built, ships had trouble going from one area of elevation to another in the region. They had to take a detour of 7.5 miles (12 kilometers) to get to a structure that would lift the boats to a higher elevation so they could continue their journey. The new aqueduct saves boats time and connects Berlin's network of harbors with ports along the Rhine River.

Shown here is the Magdeburg Water Bridge. Boats can sail on the upper and lower parts.

## A Cool but Impractical Idea

The distance from Alaska to Russia is about 55 miles (88.5 km) across the Bering Strait. It would be easy to build a bridge spanning this distance, especially since there are two small islands called the Diomedes in between that could serve as anchor points. However, there are several reasons why this bridge is not likely to ever be built. One is the climate. In this part of the world, temperatures can drop to -58 degrees Fahrenheit (-50 degrees Celsius) in the winter. For their own safety, a construction crew would only be able to work on the bridge during the summer. Furthermore, although it sounds cool to be able to drive from the United States to Europe or Asia, it would take weeks. It is likely most people would choose not to use the bridge when they could simply take a plane and arrive in hours.

Another problem is that the area near the Bering Strait is mostly uninhabited on both sides. On the Alaska side alone, 520 miles (836 km) of new roads would need to be built to connect the city of Fairbanks with Nome, the town closest to the strait. This would cost about $5 million per mile, making the project too expensive before work even starts on the bridge.

# FUTURISTIC MATERIALS

In other areas of transportation, engineers are working to change the way things function—for example, by making cars that can fly or trains that can reach outer space. However, we will not see a hovering bridge any time soon. Instead, engineers are focusing their energy on new materials that will help them build better, longer-lasting bridges. Carbon nanotubes are stronger and lighter than steel, which means that in the future, engineers will be able to build bridges that are even longer than the ones they can make right now.

Some engineers are working on using 3-D printing to make replaceable parts for bridges. This would let them swap damaged pieces out quickly and easily, the way mechanics can replace parts of a car when they wear out. In the future, robots might be able to replace these parts, which would make bridge repair much less dangerous for humans.

Another amazing material that is already in limited use is called self-healing concrete. This kind of concrete can actually repair cracks on its own! To make it, people mix certain kinds of bacteria into the concrete. These bacteria can live up to 200 years, but they stay **dormant** until cracks in the concrete allow air to get in. At that point, the bacteria start feeding on oxygen and some of the concrete materials. They **excrete** similar materials, which bind with the existing concrete to seal the crack. Self-healing concrete can make bridges last much longer by allowing them to make their own minor repairs before the problems get too big. However, as of 2022, it is much more expensive to use than regular concrete. This adds a lot to a project's initial price tag, which is why not everyone can afford to use it.

Another way to make concrete high-tech is to put electric sensors in it. These sensors send information about a bridge's condition to engineers' computers. This lets engineers know about problems immediately. Making repairs while the problem is still small is much cheaper than waiting until they get so big that the bridge has to be closed for safety reasons.

# STYLISH BRIDGES

Pedestrian bridges have the ability to be even more spectacular than bridges for trains or cars. This is because they do not have to be as long or hold as heavy a load. The Henderson Waves Bridge in Singapore is one example of creative bridge design.

Shown here is the Henderson Waves Bridge. At night, the bridge lights up, making it glow softly among the trees.

It connects parts of the city that are separated by major roads and dense trees. Because it rises high above the trees, it makes sightseeing easy. The bridge gets part of its name from the fact that it looks wavy, dipping and rising. The parts that rise up cover benches to provide shade and rest for pedestrians. The lighting on the bridge makes it look beautiful even at night.

Ponte Vecchio in Florence, Italy, is not a futuristic bridge; in fact, it was built in the 14th century, and its name literally means "old bridge" in Italian. However, it is one of the most unique bridges in the world. For one thing, it was the first **segmented** arch bridge to be built in Europe, and it is still standing today. The segmented design needs fewer support beams in the middle of Florence's Arno River, which allows more room for boats. Additionally, as of 2022, it is one of only four bridges in the world to have shops on it! Another of these bridges is the Krämerbrücke bridge in Erfurt, Germany. About 80 people actually call this bridge their home, since there are living quarters above many of the shops. As concerns about flooding due to climate change grow, some people have suggested that living on bridges could be a solution. With the improved materials available today, this might become a popular style of housing in the future.

# THINK IT THROUGH

1. What issues do you think engineers had to address to design the Magdeburg Water Bridge?

2. Why do you think self-healing concrete is more expensive than regular concrete?

3. What challenges might creating houses on a bridge present for engineers?

Shown here is Ponte Vecchio. In the future, living and shopping on a bridge may not seem so unusual.

# GLOSSARY

**aggregate:** A mass or body of units or parts.

**civilian:** A person who is not in a military, police, or firefighting unit.

**dormant:** Not active but able to become active.

**emissions:** Substances that are discharged into the air.

**excrete:** To pass waste matter from the body.

**frequency:** The number of waves of sound or energy that pass by a point every second.

**girder:** A large beam used for bridge building.

**nanotube:** A microscopic tube whose diameter is measured in nanometers.

**pedestrian:** A person who is walking.

**pile:** A heavy post or stake that supports a large structure.

**prototype:** An original or first model of something from which other forms are copied.

**reinforce:** To strengthen something by adding more material for support.

**segmented:** Divided into sections.

**sustainable:** Able to be maintained for a long time.

**thermodynamics:** The branch of science that has to do with heat and energy.

# FIND OUT MORE

## Books

Bell, Samantha. *Bridges*. New York, NY: Smartbook Media, 2019.

Noyce, Pendred. *Engineering Bridges: Connecting the World*. Boston, MA: Tumblehome, 2019.

Spray, Sally, and Mark Ruffle. *Bridges*. London, UK: Franklin Watts, 2019.

## Websites

**BrainPOP: Bridges**
*www.brainpop.com/technology/ scienceandindustry/bridges*
Watch videos and take quizzes to learn more about bridges.

**PBS: Bridge Basics**
*www.pbs.org/wgbh/buildingbig/ bridge*
This website gives information about bridge basics and famous bridges around the world. It also includes a bridge-building game.

## Organizations

**American Society of Civil Engineers (ASCE)**
1801 Alexander Bell Drive
Reston, VA 20191
Email: customercare@asce.org
*asce.org*
This organization connects civil engineers across the United States. ASCE also hosts a yearly Concrete Canoe Competition to give engineering students hands-on experience in concrete mixing and project management.

**National Society for the Preservation of Covered Bridges**
535 Second NH Turnpike
Hillsboro, NH 03244
Email: nspcb@yahoo.com
*www.coveredbridgesociety.org*
As its name suggests, this group works to keep America's historic covered bridges in good condition.

# INDEX

**P**

Ponte Vecchio, 42–43

**S**

sensors, 41

steel, 7, 13, 19, 24, 26, 29,
31–33, 40

suspension bridges, 14–15,
22, 24, 26–27

**T**

Tacoma Narrows Bridge, 22, 27

tension, 9–10

3-D printing, 20, 40

trusses, 13–14, 19

**V**

vibrations, 24–25, 27

**W**

water, 6–7, 9, 12, 16, 23–24,
32, 38

# ABOUT THE AUTHOR

**SOPHIE WASHBURNE** has been a freelance writer and editor of young adult and adult books for more than 10 years. She travels extensively with her husband, Alan. When they are not traveling, they live in Wales with their cat, Zoe. Sophie enjoys doing crafts and cooking when she has spare time. She would like to thank Kyle Eudene for his invaluable contributions to this book.